POP CLASSICS FOR TWO

Arrangements by Mark Phillips

ISBN 978-1-5400-6533-9

Visit Hal Leonard Online at
www.halleonard.com

Contact us:
Hal Leonard
7777 West Bluemound Road
Milwaukee, WI 53213
Email: info@halleonard.com

In Europe, contact:
Hal Leonard Europe Limited
42 Wigmore Street
Marylebone, London, W1U 2RN
Email: info@halleonardeurope.com

In Australia, contact:
Hal Leonard Australia Pty. Ltd.
4 Lentara Court
Cheltenham, Victoria, 3192 Australia
Email: info@halleonard.com.au

AFRICA

FLUTES

Words and Music by DAVID PAICH
and JEFF PORCARO

Play 3 times

To Coda ⊕

2nd time, D.S. al Coda
(take repeats)

CODA
⊕

ALONE

FLUTES

Words and Music by BILLY STEINBERG
and TOM KELLY

CAN'T SMILE WITHOUT YOU

Flutes

Words and Music by CHRIS ARNOLD,
DAVID MARTIN and GEOFF MORROW

CENTERFOLD

FLUTES

Words and Music by
SETH JUSTMAN

Moderately

DANCING QUEEN

FLUTES

Words and Music by BENNY ANDERSSON,
BJÖRN ULVAEUS and STIG ANDERSON

DUST IN THE WIND

FLUTES

Words and Music by
KERRY LIVGREN

EVERY BREATH YOU TAKE

FLUTES

Words and Music by
STING

EYE OF THE TIGER

Theme from ROCKY III

Flutes

Words and Music by FRANK SULLIVAN
and JIM PETERIK

I MELT WITH YOU

Words and Music by RICHARD IAN BROWN,
MICHAEL FRANCIS CONROY, ROBERT JAMES GREY,
GARY FRANCES McDOWELL and STEPHEN JAMES WALKER

Flutes

I STILL HAVEN'T FOUND WHAT I'M LOOKING FOR

FLUTES

Words and Music by
U2

IMAGINE

FLUTES

Words and Music by
JOHN LENNON

Moderately slow

JESSIE'S GIRL

FLUTES

Words and Music by
RICK SPRINGFIELD

LEAN ON ME

FLUTES

Words and Music by
BILL WITHERS

PIANO MAN

FLUTES

Words and Music by
BILLY JOEL

RIGHT HERE WAITING

FLUTES

Words and Music by
RICHARD MARX

SILLY LOVE SONGS

FLUTES

Words and Music by PAUL McCARTNEY
and LINDA McCARTNEY

THE SOUND OF SILENCE

FLUTES

Words and Music by
PAUL SIMON

STAND BY ME

FLUTES

Words and Music by JERRY LEIBER, MIKE STOLLER and BEN E. KING

SWEET CAROLINE

FLUTES

Words and Music by
NEIL DIAMOND

2nd time, D.C. al Coda

CODA

TAKE ON ME

FLUTES

Words by PAL WAAKTAAR
and MAGNE FURUHOLMNE
Words by PAL WAAKTAAR,
MAGNE FURUHOLMNE and MORTN HARKET

(small notes optional)

TIME AFTER TIME

FLUTES

Words and Music by CYNDI LAUPER
and ROB HYMAN

WE BUILT THIS CITY

FLUTES

Words and Music by BERNIE TAUPIN,
MARTIN PAGE, DENNIS LAMBERT
and PETER WOLF

YOU ARE SO BEAUTIFUL

FLUTES

Words and Music by BILLY PRESTON
and BRUCE FISHER

Slowly, with feeling